PORTRAITS OF THE STATES

★ ★ ★ ★ ★ ★ ★ ★ ★ ★ ★ ★ ★ ★ ★ ★ ★ ★

S0-AIQ-950

MASSACHUSETTS

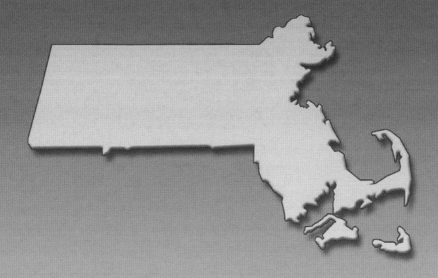

by Melissa Fairley
and Jonatha A. Brown

GARETH**STEVENS**
PUBLISHING
A Member of the WRC Media Family of Companies

Please visit our web site at: www.garethstevens.com
For a free color catalog describing Gareth Stevens Publishing's
list of high-quality books and multimedia programs, call
1-800-542-2595.

Library of Congress Cataloging-in-Publication Data

Fairley, Melissa.
    Massachusetts / Melissa Fairley and Jonatha A. Brown.
      p. cm. — (Portraits of the states)
    Includes bibliographical references and index.
    ISBN-13: 978-0-8368-4626-3 (lib. bdg.)
    ISBN-10: 0-8368-4626-5 (lib. bdg.)
    ISBN-13: 978-0-8368-4645-4 (softcover)
    ISBN-10: 0-8368-4645-1 (softcover)
    1. Massachusetts—Juvenile literature. I. Brown, Jonatha A.
    II. Title. III. Series.
    F64.3.F35   2005
    974.4—dc22   2005042611

This North American edition first published in 2006 by
Weekly Reader Books
An imprint of Gareth Stevens Publishing
200 First Stamford Place
Stamford, CT 06912 USA

This edition copyright © 2006 by Gareth Stevens, Inc.

Editorial direction: Mark J. Sachner
Project manager: Jonatha A. Brown
Editor: Betsy Rasmussen
Art direction and design: Tammy West
Picture research: Diane Laska-Swanke
Indexer: Walter Kronenberg
Production: Jessica Morris and Robert Kraus

Picture credits: Cover, © CORBIS; pp. 4, 6, 17, 22 © Gibson Stock Photography;
pp. 5, 19 © PhotoDisc; pp. 7, 10, 20, 24, 25 © Corel; p. 8 © Mansell/Time &
Life Pictures/Getty Images; p. 12 © Library of Congress; p. 15 © Alfred
Eisenstaedt/Time & Life Pictures/Getty Images; p. 26 © Michael Springer/Getty
Images; p. 28 © David Drapkin/Getty Images

Printed in the United States of America

2 3 4 5 6 7 8 9 10 09 08 07

CONTENTS

Words that are defined in the Glossary appear
in **bold** the first time they are used in the text.

On the Cover: The city of Boston lies along the Charles River.

Introduction

Massachusetts is a small state with a big place in U.S. history. Early white settlers lived along its coast. Men and women fought for freedom on its farmlands. People from Massachusetts helped shape a new nation.

Massachusetts is just as lively today as it was long ago. It has the great city of Boston and the soft sandy beaches of Cape Cod. It has living history museums and famous sports teams. It has street festivals, great music, and much more. There is so much to see and do in Massachusetts, it's hard to choose where to go first!

Martha's Vineyard draws tourists and boaters to its lovely shores.

The state flag of Massachusetts.

MASSACHUSETTS FACTS

- Became the 6th State: February 6, 1788
- Population (2004): 6,416,505
- Capital: Boston
- Biggest Cities: Boston, Worcester, Springfield, Lowell
- Size: 7,840 square miles (20,306 square kilometers)
- Nickname: The Bay State
- State Tree: American elm
- State Flower: Mayflower
- State Cat and Dog: Tabby cat,
  Boston terrier
- State Bird: Black-capped chickadee

History

The first Native Americans came to Massachusetts thousands of years ago. They hunted big animals for food. Back then, the area was colder than it is now. Over many years, it grew warmer. More Natives arrived. They hunted turkeys and deer. They caught fish and gathered wild plants. They began growing corn, beans, and squash. By 1600, seven different tribes lived in Massachusetts.

The First Europeans

No one knows when the first Europeans arrived. Explorers from Norway may have landed on Cape Cod one thousand years ago. Men from other parts of Europe came in the early 1600s.

The **Pilgrims** were the first Europeans to settle in Massachusetts. They sailed from Great Britain in 1620. Their ship

When early Natives lived in Massachusetts, forests covered the land. Mt. Greylock is still heavily wooded today.

was named the *Mayflower*. They founded the **colony** of Plymouth. Ten years later, the Puritans came. They set up the Massachusetts Bay Colony.

Colonial Times

In 1691, the king of Britain claimed the two colonies. He combined them into one. Now the whole area was known as the Massachusetts Bay Colony. It reached as far as Maine. The king also

FUN FACTS

The Name Game

Massachusetts is named after a Native people, the Massachuset. The name means "near the great hill" or "large hill place." The Massachusets lived near Great Blue Hill. This hill is just south of Boston.

This ship is a copy of the *Mayflower*, the ship that brought the first Pilgrims to Plymouth, Massachusetts.

FUN FACTS

The First Thanksgiving

Many Pilgrims died during their first winter. They did not have enough food. In the spring, friendly Natives gave them seeds to plant. In the fall, the Pilgrims and the Natives had a great harvest feast. It was the first Thanksgiving.

IN MASSACHUSETTS'S HISTORY

Pilgrims Agree

As the Pilgrims sailed over the ocean, they talked about how they would govern themselves. They agreed that their laws should be good for all of the people, not just the rich and strong. They wrote their laws down. Their list of ideas and laws became the Mayflower **Compact**.

The Road to Revolution

The fighting had cost a great deal of money. Now, the British king wanted the colonists to pay a part of the cost of the war. To get money from them, he put **taxes** on supplies that were

claimed other colonies along the coast.

The French wanted some of this land, too. They went to war against Britain. In 1763, the British won the war.

Colonists threw crates of tea into the harbor during the Boston Tea Party.

sent to the colonies. Some colonists said the taxes were not fair. In Boston, fights began to break out between angry colonists and British soldiers.

In 1773, the British said that only one company could sell tea in the colonies. Many colonists did not like this rule. Some of them decided to take action. When a ship loaded with tea sailed into Boston Harbor, the colonists sneaked aboard. They dumped the tea over the side and into the water. Now, it could not be sold to anyone. This was called the Boston Tea Party.

The British tried to teach the colonists a lesson. They closed Boston Harbor. They passed laws that made life even harder for the colonists. British soldiers moved into the homes of the colonists. The colonists were shocked and angered.

Famous People of Massachusetts

Samuel Adams

Born: September 27, 1722, Boston, Massachusetts

Died: October 3, 1803, Boston, Massachusetts

Samuel Adams was a **patriot**. He spoke out against the king's taxes. He urged the colonists to stand up to the British and helped plan the Boston Tea Party. In 1775, British soldiers tried to catch Adams. They marched to Lexington to find him, but Adams escaped. This led to the first battles of the Revolutionary War. In 1776, Adams signed the Declaration of Independence. After the war, he became governor of Massachusetts.

In June 1775, the colonists fought the British on a hill near Boston. The fight was called the Battle of Bunker Hill.

The problems got worse. On April 19, 1775, the British marched toward Concord. They planned to surprise the colonists. They wanted to take away their guns and catch their leaders. But the colonists found out about the plan. Paul Revere and William Dawes jumped on their horses and dashed off to warn people.

The Fight for Freedom

The British got as far as Lexington. There, they met a group of colonists. Shots were fired, and a few colonists were killed. The soldiers marched on to Concord. When they arrived, armed colonists attacked them. The colonists beat the British back. These battles marked the start of the Revolutionary War.

The war lasted for eight years. Many battles were

fought in Massachusetts. Finally, the colonists won. They formed a new country, the United States of America. In 1788, Massachusetts became the sixth state.

The Growth of Factories

As the new nation grew, the state grew, too. In 1814, the world's first **textile** mill opened. It was in the city of Waltham. At this mill, machines spun cotton into yarn and wove yarn into cloth. A new period in history began. Machines did more and more work. People did less and less work by hand.

Factories sprang up in Massachusetts. They made textiles, shoes, and paper. These goods were shipped to markets far away, so shipping also grew. People also hunted whales for their oil.

The Fight against Slavery

In the early 1800s, people in the state began to speak out against slavery. Other states in the North agreed that slavery was wrong. But people in the South said they needed African American slaves to make money.

The South broke away from the North and formed a new country. The northern states did not want two countries. The two sides began to fight in 1861. This was the Civil War.

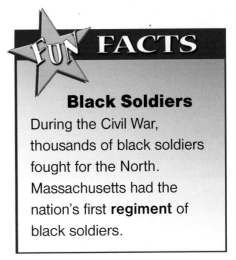

FUN FACTS

Black Soldiers

During the Civil War, thousands of black soldiers fought for the North. Massachusetts had the nation's first **regiment** of black soldiers.

The North won. The North and South were one country again. Slavery was now against the law.

Ups and Downs

During the late 1800s and early 1900s, people flooded into the state. They were drawn by the many jobs in the factories.

But many companies left Massachusetts in the early 1900s. They moved south or west, where labor was cheaper. All over the state, workers lost their jobs. Years passed before new kinds of businesses came to Massachusetts. They created many new jobs.

IN MASSACHUSETTS'S HISTORY

Going Under

The first underground railway, or **subway**, in the United States opened in Boston in 1897. It was 1.5 miles (2.4 km) long.

Today, Massachusetts is an important center for **high-tech** business. Many Internet companies have settled in the western part of the state. The state is also the home of well-known **political** leaders. One is Senator John Kerry. He ran for president in 2004.

Many years ago, thousands of factory workers in Massachusetts posed for this old photo.

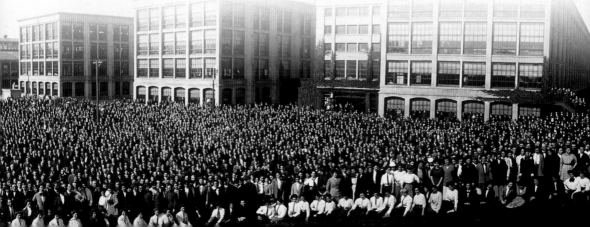

1620	Pilgrims arrive on the *Mayflower*.
1691	The area becomes part of the Massachusetts Bay Colony.
1763	Britain wins a war with France and takes full control of thirteen American colonies, including Massachusetts.
1773	Colonists dump tea into the harbor in an event called the Boston Tea Party.
1775	The Revolutionary War begins in Lexington and Concord.
1788	Massachusetts becomes the sixth state.
1814	The world's first textile mill opens in Waltham.
1861–1865	Massachusetts sides with the North in the Civil War.
Late 1800s– Early 1900s	People from all over the world move to Massachusetts.
1897	The first subway in the United States opens in Boston.
1960	John F. Kennedy, senator from Massachusetts, is elected president.
2004	Senator John Kerry from Massachusetts loses the presidential election to George W. Bush.

People

More than six million people live in Massachusetts. They come from many backgrounds. They and their families come from all over the world.

The first people to live in the state were Native Americans. Later, settlers from Britain arrived. Very few Natives live in the state today. Many people whose families first came from Britain still live in Massachusetts.

Hispanics: In the 2000 U.S. Census, 6.8 percent of the people living in Massachusetts called themselves Latino or Hispanic. Most of them or their relatives came from places where Spanish is spoken. They may come from different racial backgrounds.

The People of Massachusetts

Total Population 6,416,505

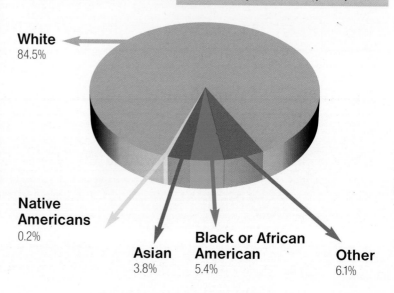

White
84.5%

Native Americans
0.2%

Asian
3.8%

Black or African American
5.4%

Other
6.1%

Percentages are based on the 2000 Census.

John F. Kennedy

Born: May 29, 1917, Brookline, Massachusetts

Died: November 22, 1963, Dallas, Texas

John F. Kennedy came from an Irish American family. As a young man, he was a war hero. Later, he became the youngest man ever to be elected U.S. president. He was also the first Catholic to be elected president. When he became president, he inspired many people to work hard for others. He said, "Ask not what your country can do for you; ask what you can do for your country." He was shot and killed two and one-half years later.

John F. Kennedy of Massachusetts was the thirty-fifth president of the United States.

The first African Americans in Massachusetts were slaves. Slavery was outlawed in Massachusetts in 1783. After that, many black people stayed in the state as free women and men. In the South, slaves ran away from slave owners. Some made their way to Massachusetts. Today, about 5 percent of the people in the state are African American.

Massachusetts had plenty of jobs at factories and mills in the 1800s. The work was hard, the hours were long, and the pay was low. But many people from other countries were glad to have these jobs in order to get started in the United States.

15

Back then, many men, women, and children came from Ireland to work in the mills. Later, people came from Italy. Today, many people whose families came from Ireland and Italy still live in the state.

Lately, more people have come from places where Spanish is spoken. These places include Cuba, Puerto Rico, and the Dominican Republic. Massachusetts is also home to people from all over Europe and Asia.

Famous People of Massachusetts

John Adams

Born: October 30, 1735, Braintree, Massachusetts
Died: July 4, 1826, Quincy, Massachusetts

John Adams was the second president of the United States. He went to Harvard University. He then became a lawyer in the Massachesetts Bay Colony. Adams wanted the colonies to be free from Britain. He helped work out a treaty that ended the Revolutionary War. Adams served as vice president under George Washington before becoming president himself. He was the first president to live in the White House.

John Quincy Adams

Born: July 11, 1767, Braintree, Massachusetts
Died: February 23, 1848, Washington, D.C.

John Quincy Adams was the first president who was the son of another president. He was the sixth president of the United States. John Quincy Adams wanted to connect the nation with roads and canals. He thought the country should pay for scientific exploring. After his presidency, he became a powerful leader in Congress.

Harvard University was founded in 1636 in Cambridge. Today, it is famous around the world.

Most people in the state of Massachusetts live in or near cities. Boston is the largest city. Few people live on farms in Massachusetts these days.

Education

In 1635, the first public school in the U.S. colonies opened in Boston. In 1647, the government decided that most villages had to have schools. By 1840, the whole state had a public school system.

These days, the state is known for its fine colleges.

Harvard is the oldest college in the nation. It is also one of the best. The Massachusetts Institute of Technology is another well-known university. Mount Holyoke was one of the first colleges in the country for women.

Religion

Most people in the state are Christians. Of these, the majority are Protestants, just as the Pilgrims were. Nearly one-third of the people there are Catholics. A smaller number of Jews and people of other religions also live in Massachusetts.

17

The Land

Thousands of years ago, Massachusetts was covered by huge sheets of ice. That time is known as the **Ice Age**. When the ice melted, it left behind huge piles of rock and sand. Some of the largest piles formed Cape Cod and the islands of Martha's Vineyard and Nantucket.

The ice shaped most of the state's coastline along the Atlantic Ocean. It also dug out dozens of lakes and dumped huge boulders across the land.

The Lay of the Land

The land in eastern Massachusetts is made up of low, rolling hills and waterways. There are swamps, lakes, rivers, and ponds.

Famous People of Massachusetts

Henry David Thoreau

Born: July 12, 1817, Concord, Massachusetts

Died: May 6, 1862, Concord, Massachusetts

Thoreau was a writer. One of his most famous books was *Walden*. In this book, he wrote about a year when he lived in a small shack in the woods. During that time, he lived simply. He explored and enjoyed the natural beauty around him. People still like to read *Walden* today.

MASSACHUSETTS

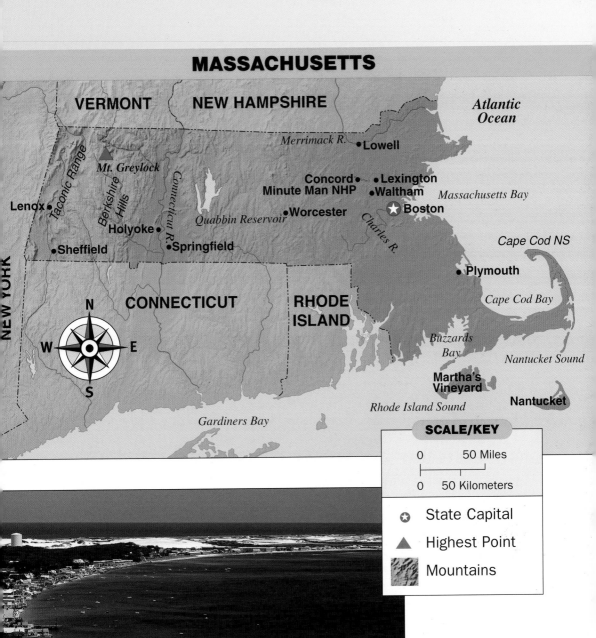

VERMONT   NEW HAMPSHIRE

Atlantic Ocean

Merrimack R. • Lowell

Mt. Greylock

Taconic Range

Berkshire Hills

Connecticut R.

Concord •   • Lexington
Minute Man NHP   • Waltham

Massachusetts Bay

Lenox •

☆ Boston

Quabbin Reservoir • Worcester

Holyoke •

Charles R.

Cape Cod NS

• Sheffield   • Springfield

• Plymouth

NEW YORK

N
W   E
S

CONNECTICUT

RHODE ISLAND

Cape Cod Bay

Buzzards Bay

Nantucket Sound

Martha's Vineyard

Nantucket

Rhode Island Sound

Gardiners Bay

SCALE/KEY

0   50 Miles

0   50 Kilometers

⊛   State Capital

▲   Highest Point

  Mountains

The sandy beaches of Cape Cod stretch out into the Atlantic Ocean.

The land in the middle of the state is hilly. In the west, the Connecticut River cuts through the hills. The flat land along the river is good for farming.

Mountains stand in the western part of the state. Forests cover them. Mount Greylock is in this area. At 3,491 feet (1,064 meters), it is the state's highest peak.

Lakes and Rivers

Many rivers flow across Massachusetts. The Connecticut River is the

Pheasants live in open fields all over Massachusetts.

Major Rivers

Connecticut River
407 miles (655 km) long

Merrimack River
110 miles (177 km) long

Charles River
80 miles (130 km) long

longest. It runs through Massachusetts and other nearby states.

More than eleven hundred lakes and ponds dot the land. The largest lake is Quabbin **Reservoir**. To make this lake, workers flooded five towns along the Swift River. Now it provides drinking water to people in many cities and towns.

Plants and Animals

More than half of Massachusetts is covered with forests. Maple, birch, pine, and many other kinds

Different plants grow along the coast. Tufts of grass pop up from the sand dunes. Short, twisted pine and oak trees grow there, too. Beach roses bloom all summer long.

The fields and woods of Massachusetts are home to deer, foxes, beavers, and many small animals. Skunks, chipmunks, and raccoons are common. Some bears and moose still live in the state. They are found mostly in the western mountains.

of trees grow there. Some of them lose their leaves in the fall of each year. Just before the leaves drop, they turn bright red, orange, or yellow. It is beautiful to see.

Wildflowers bloom in early spring. Red trillium, violets, and bloodroot can be found then. A few weeks later, many shrubs and bushes flower. The pink mountain laurel and white dogwoods put on a show then, too.

Herons and egrets live in the swamps and near ponds. Ducks and loons make their nests near the ponds and lakes, too. Sandpipers and gulls hunt for food on beaches along the ocean. Bobwhites, kingfishers, warblers, and other birds fly over the land.

21

Economy

Long ago, most people in Massachusetts were farmers. Some built ships or caught fish for a living. Later, many people worked in factories. Massachusetts was home to many of the nation's early factories.

Fishing has long been a way of life for some people in Massachusetts.

Today, some people still fish or farm for a living. Massachusetts' farmers grow lots of cranberries. Fishing is still a major industry in the state. Other people work in factories. But most people today work

in offices. Many have **high-tech** jobs. Some of these workers design computers. Others write new computer programs.

Many people have jobs that help other people in the state. These are called service jobs. Some service workers are doctors or teachers. Others work in banks or grocery stores. Still others build houses or provide homes and offices with electric power or phone service. And many keep buildings clean and repaired.

Tourism also creates many jobs. People who visit Massachusetts stay in hotels. They eat in restaurants. They visit museums and other historic places. They hike in the Berkshire Hills or relax on Cape Cod beaches. All of these places need workers to keep tourist businesses running.

How Money Is Made in Massachusetts

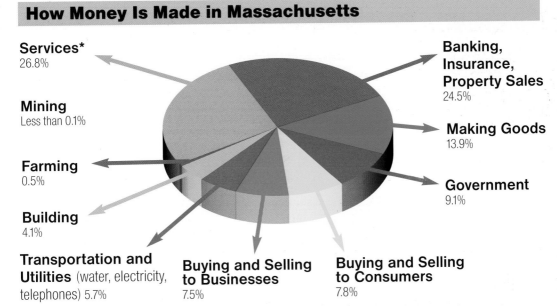

Services*
26.8%

Mining
Less than 0.1%

Farming
0.5%

Building
4.1%

Banking, Insurance, Property Sales
24.5%

Making Goods
13.9%

Government
9.1%

Transportation and Utilities (water, electricity, telephones) 5.7%

Buying and Selling to Businesses
7.5%

Buying and Selling to Consumers
7.8%

* Services include jobs in hotels, restaurants, auto repair, medicine, teaching, and entertainment.

Government

Boston is the capital of Massachusetts. The leaders of the state work there. The state government has three parts, or branches. They are the executive, legislative, and judicial branches.

Executive Branch

The executive branch carries out the state's laws. The governor is the leader of this branch. A lieutenant governor helps. A team of people called the **cabinet** also works for the governor.

The Boston State House was built in 1789. It is the state capitol building.

The state House of Representatives meets in this large hall.

Legislative Branch

The legislative branch is called the General Court. It has two parts — the House of Representatives and the Senate. Their jobs are to make laws for the state.

Judicial Branch

Judges and courts make up the judicial branch. Judges **interpret** state laws. They may decide whether some-one who is **accused of** committing a crime is guilty.

Local Government

In Massachusetts, some towns are run by a mayor. Others are run by a group of town officials. Many towns hold town meetings. Voters go to these meetings to talk about important matters facing the town and to express their feelings.

MASSACHUSETTS'S STATE GOVERNMENT

Executive		Legislative		Judicial	
Office	Length of Term	Body	Length of Term	Court	Length of Term
Governor	4 years	Senate (40 members)	4 years	Supreme (7 justices)	Appointed by governor, serve until age 70
Lieutenant Governor	4 years	House of Representatives (160 members)	2 years	Appeals (25 justices)	Appointed by governor, serve until age 70

Things to See and Do

People come to Massachusetts for many reasons. In spring, visitors hike in its mountains and forests. In summer, they swim at the beaches. In autumn, they look at brightly colored leaves. All year long, they visit the state's many museums and the Cape Cod National Seashore.

A trip to Plimoth Plantation is like a trip back in time. Guides at this museum dress like the Pilgrims did.

Remembering the Past

Massachusetts's history museums bring the past alive. In Plymouth, visitors can see a ship that looks just like the *Mayflower*. In Boston, they can walk the Freedom Trail and see Paul Revere's house. In Lexington, they can visit the bedroom where Samuel Adams slept the night before the Revolutionary War started.

Plimoth Plantation and Old Sturbridge Village are living-history museums. Actors dress and speak like the early settlers in Massachusetts. They show visitors how people lived and worked long ago.

A Place for the Arts

For people who love art and music, Massachusetts is an exciting place. On warm summer nights, visitors hear orchestras play at Tanglewood in Lenox. They go to Sheffield to watch actors perform plays on a stage.

Famous People of Massachusetts

Sharon Christa McAuliffe

Born: September 2, 1948, Boston, Massachusetts

Died: January 28, 1986, off Cape Canaveral, Florida

Christa McAuliffe was a teacher who liked to take her classes on field trips. In 1984, she was chosen to be the first teacher to travel into space. It was to be a very exciting event. Sadly, something went very wrong. Less than two minutes after lift off, the space shuttle *Challenger* blew up. McAuliffe and the other people on the shuttle died.

Boston is full of art and music all year long. It is home to the Museum of Fine Arts. This museum has many wonderful paintings and all kinds of art on display. The state is also

FACTS

New Games

Both basketball and volley-ball were invented in Massachusetts. Basketball was first played in Springfield. Volleyball got its start in Holyoke. Both were invented in the late 1800s.

The New England Patriots score in the Super Bowl of 2005. The Patriots beat the Philadelphia Eagles, 24-21.

home to the Children's Museum, which was one of the first museums to use hands-on displays. The city also hosts outdoor concerts and music festivals.

Sports

Massachusetts is home to five big-league sports teams. The Boston Celtics basketball team has won more NBA **championships** than any other basketball team. The state's football team, the New England Patriots, won the Super Bowl in 2005. In 2004, the Boston Red Sox won the World Series. Fans also enjoy watching the New England Revolution play soccer and the Boston Bruins play hockey.

Famous People of Massachusetts

Dr. Seuss

Born: March 2, 1904, Springfield, Massachusetts

Died: September 24, 1991, La Jolla, California

Dr. Seuss's real name was Theodore Geisel. He saw that many children had trouble learning to read. He also saw that most children's books were boring or used too many words. He decided to write a book using just 250 words. The result was *The Cat in the Hat*. It was a funny book, and kids loved it. Soon, he wrote more books for young children. Some of them were *Green Eggs and Ham, How the Grinch Stole Christmas*, and *Horton Hears a Who*. His books made Dr. Seuss famous.

★ ★

accused of — blamed for

cabinet — a team of people who help a political leader make decisions

championships — games played between the two best teams in a sport

colony — a group of people living in a new land but keeping ties with the country they came from

compact — an agreement between people or groups of people

high-tech — having to do with computers

Ice Age — a period when great sheets of ice covered most of North America

interpret — explain what something means

patriot — a person who loves his or her country

Pilgrims — in 1620, a group of people who came to Massachusetts from Britain

political — having to do with governing

regiment — a large group of soldiers

reservoir — an artificial lake where water is stored for later use

subway — an underground railway

taxes — money one must pay the government sometimes when buying something

textile — cloth

tourism — traveling for pleasure

Books

Clambake: A Wampanoag Tradition. We Are Still Here (series)
Russell M. Peters. (Children's Press)

Daily Life in the Pilgrim Colony 1636. Paul Erickson.
(Clarion Books)

Henry David's House. Henry David Thoreau and
Steven Schnur. (Charlesbridge Publishing)

Journey around Boston from A to Z. Journey Around A to Z
(series) Martha Zschock. (Commonwealth Editions)

Massachusetts. Rookie Read-About biography (series)
Sarah De Capua. (Children's Press)

Web Sites

The Freedom Trail
www.thefreedomtrail.org

Living History Museum: Seventeenth Century Plymouth
www.plimoth.org

Paul Revere's Historic House Museum
www.paulreverehouse.org

The Salem Witch Trials
www.salemwitchmuseum.org